XTREME WRESTLING ROYALTY

DWAYNE "THE ROCK" JOHNSON

A&D Xtreme
BOLD HI-LO NONFICTION
An imprint of Abdo Publishing
abdobooks.com

ALEX MONNIG

TAKE IT TO THE XTREME!

GET READY FOR AN EXTREME ADVENTURE! THE PAGES OF THIS BOOK WILL TAKE YOU INTO THE THRILLING WORLD OF PROFESSIONAL WRESTLING. WHEN YOU HAVE FINISHED READING THIS BOOK, TAKE THE XTREME CHALLENGE ON PAGE 45 ABOUT WHAT YOU'VE LEARNED!

ABDOBOOKS.COM
Published by Abdo Publishing, a division of ABDO, PO Box 398166, Minneapolis, Minnesota 55439.
Printed in the United States of America, North Mankato, MN.
052023
092023

THIS BOOK CONTAINS RECYCLED MATERIALS

Design: Kelly Doudna, Mighty Media, Inc.
Production: Mighty Media, Inc.
Editor: Katherine Chu
Cover Photograph: Megan Elice Meadows/Flickr
Interior Photographs: Alan Diaz/AP Images, pp. 14–15; Allstar Picture Library Ltd/Alamy Photo, p. 26; CelebrityArchaeology.com/Alamy Photo, p. 5; Ed Webster/Flickr, pp. 36–37; EDURRA/Shutterstock Images, pp. 6–7; Elliott Cowand Jr/Shutterstock Images, p. 41; Gavin Rodgers/Alamy Photo, pp. 18–19; George Pimentel/Getty Images, pp. 34–35; Hlib Shabashnyi/Shutterstock Images, p. 10; Joseph Sohm/Shutterstock Images, pp. 4–5; Kathy Hutchins/Shutterstock Images, pp. 8–9, 40, 42–43; MandyJC72/Flickr, p. 23; Megan Elice Meadows/Flickr, pp. 12–13, 20–21, 24–25, 32–33, 44; Miguel Discart/Flickr, pp. 16–17, 27, 28, 29, 30–31; Newspix/Getty Images, p. 11; Simon Q/Flickr, pp. 22, 38–39; Tinseltown/Shutterstock Images, p. 1; Wikimedia Commons, p. 43
Design Elements: amgun/Shutterstock Images (perspective); sanchesnet1/iStockphoto (spikes color, bolts); Wth/Shutterstock Images (stripes)

LIBRARY OF CONGRESS CONTROL NUMBER: 2022948817

PUBLISHER'S CATALOGING-IN-PUBLICATION DATA
Names: Monnig, Alex, author.
Title: Dwayne "The Rock" Johnson / by Alex Monnig
Description: Minneapolis, Minnesota : Abdo Publishing, 2024 | Series: Xtreme wrestling royalty | Includes online resources and index.
Identifiers: ISBN 9781098291464 (lib. bdg.) | ISBN 9781098277925 (ebook)
Subjects: LCSH: Johnson, Dwayne, 1972---Juvenile literature. | Wrestlers--Biography--Juvenile literature. | Actors--Biography--Juvenile literature. | World Wrestling Entertainment, Inc--Juvenile literature.
Classification: DDC 796.812092--dc23

TABLE OF CONTENTS

CHAPTER 1

FIGHTING FOR THE CHAMPIONSHIP

Dwayne "the Rock" Johnson faced Mick "Mankind" Foley during the final fight of the World Wrestling Federation's (WWF) Survivor Series event in 1998. Both wrestlers performed unbelievable **stunts** and used prop weapons against each other. The Rock finally put Mankind in a wrestling submission hold called a sharpshooter hold. The bell rang. The Rock had won! He was the new World Heavyweight Champion.

The 1998 Survivor Series was held at the Kiel Center in Missouri. It was called the Deadly Game tournament because it featured 14 famous wrestlers competing for the championship.

Between 1996 and 2000, the Rock and Mankind fought as partners and rivals in more than 80 matches.

CHAPTER 2

WRESTLING ROOTS

Dwayne Douglas Johnson was born on May 2, 1972, in Hayward, California. During his childhood, Dwayne's family moved a lot. They even stayed with his grandparents in Auckland, New Zealand, for a short time.

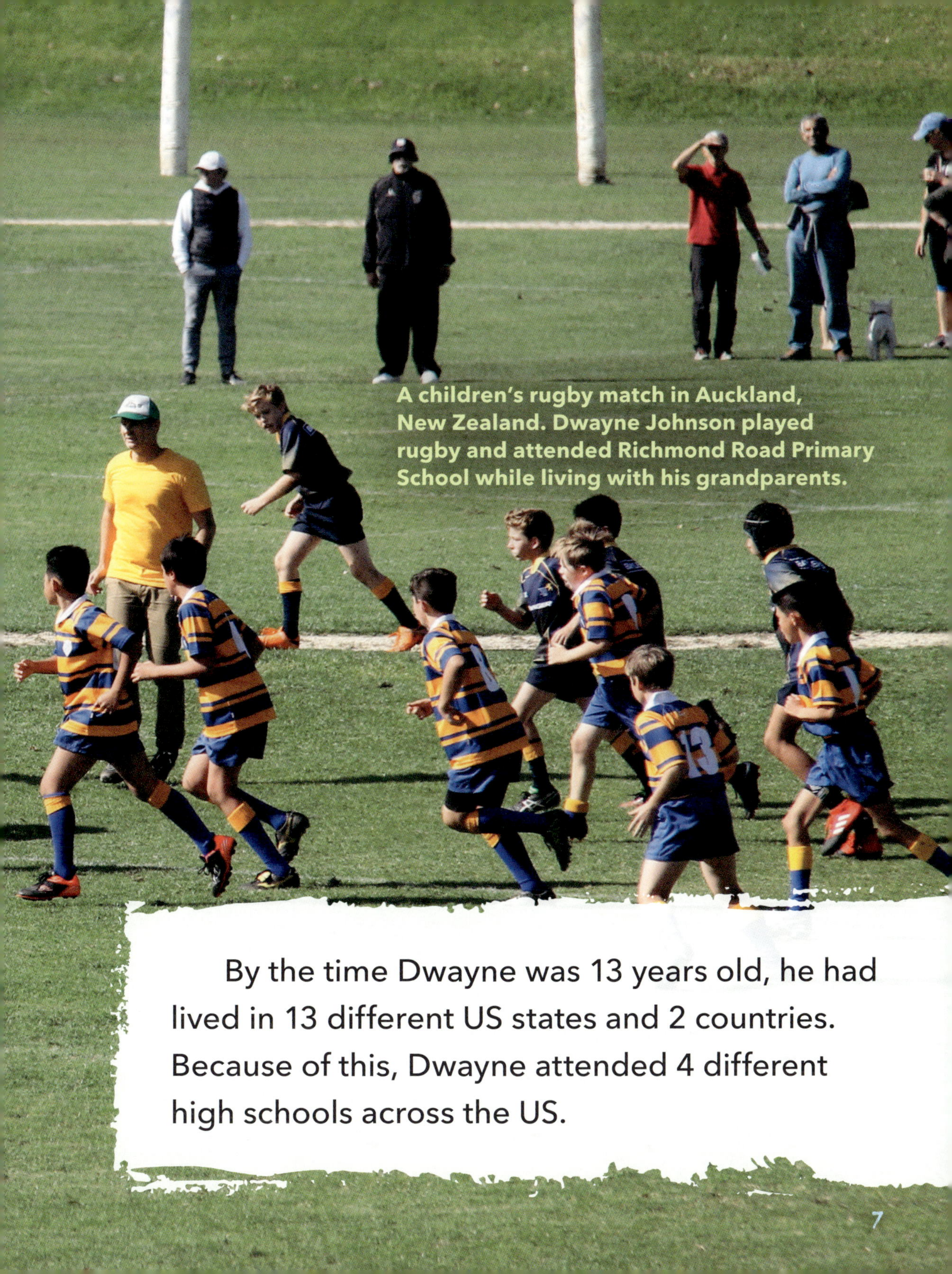

A children's rugby match in Auckland, New Zealand. Dwayne Johnson played rugby and attended Richmond Road Primary School while living with his grandparents.

By the time Dwayne was 13 years old, he had lived in 13 different US states and 2 countries. Because of this, Dwayne attended 4 different high schools across the US.

XTREME FACT

Dwayne Johnson's grandmother Lia Maivia was one of the first female professional wrestling promoters in Hawaii. She helped spread the word about events and shows.

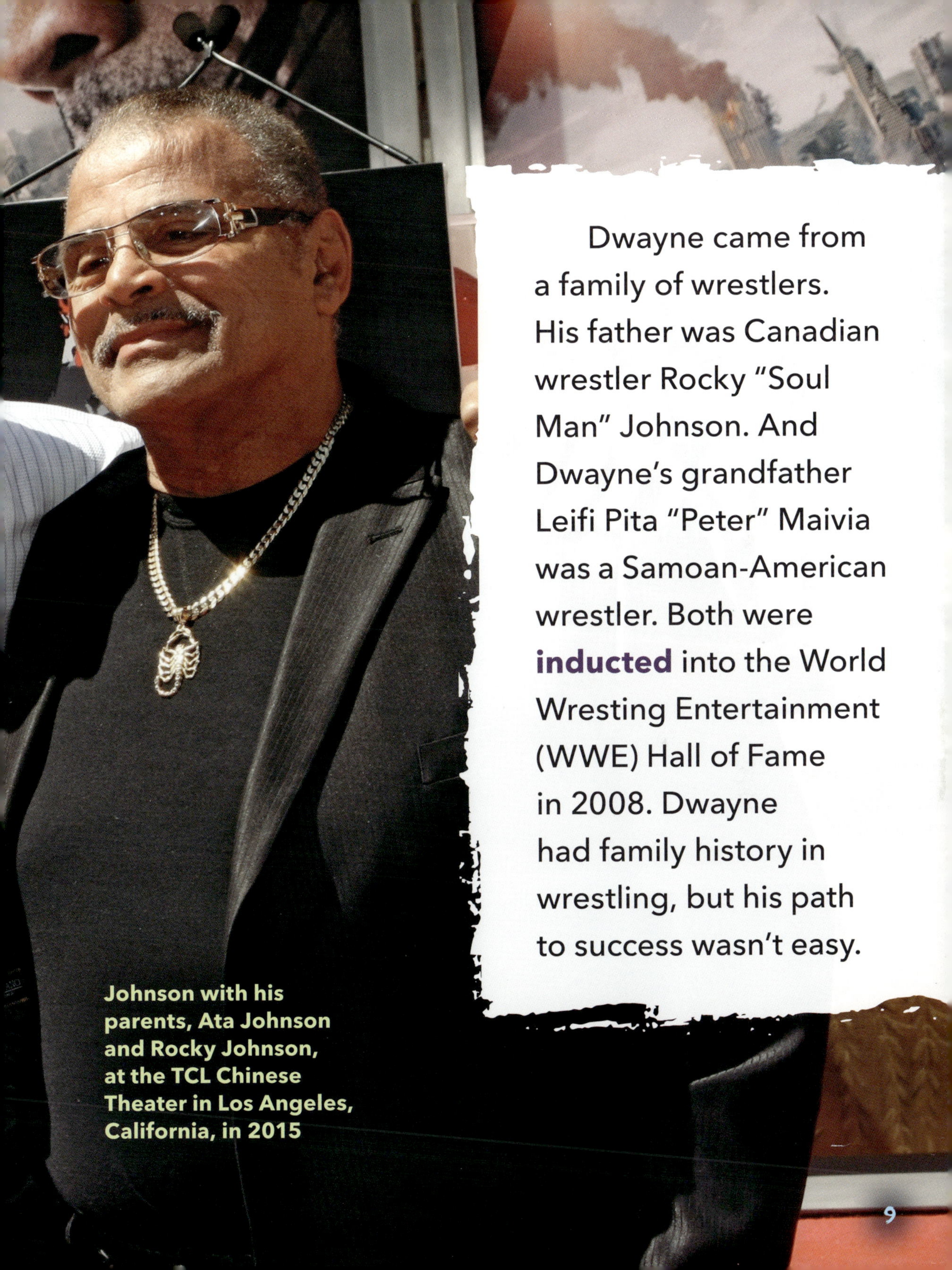

Dwayne came from a family of wrestlers. His father was Canadian wrestler Rocky "Soul Man" Johnson. And Dwayne's grandfather Leifi Pita "Peter" Maivia was a Samoan-American wrestler. Both were **inducted** into the World Wresting Entertainment (WWE) Hall of Fame in 2008. Dwayne had family history in wrestling, but his path to success wasn't easy.

Johnson with his parents, Ata Johnson and Rocky Johnson, at the TCL Chinese Theater in Los Angeles, California, in 2015

CHAPTER 3

A ROCKY START

At age 13, Dwayne started weight training. When he was 14, his family could not pay rent and were kicked out of their home. So Dwayne trained with more **determination** and purpose. He worked hard to earn enough money so he would never lose his home again.

When he was young, Dwayne learned the importance of strength and determination by watching his father and other wrestlers train for hours at the gym.

The Rock continues to work out and train as an adult to stay in shape.

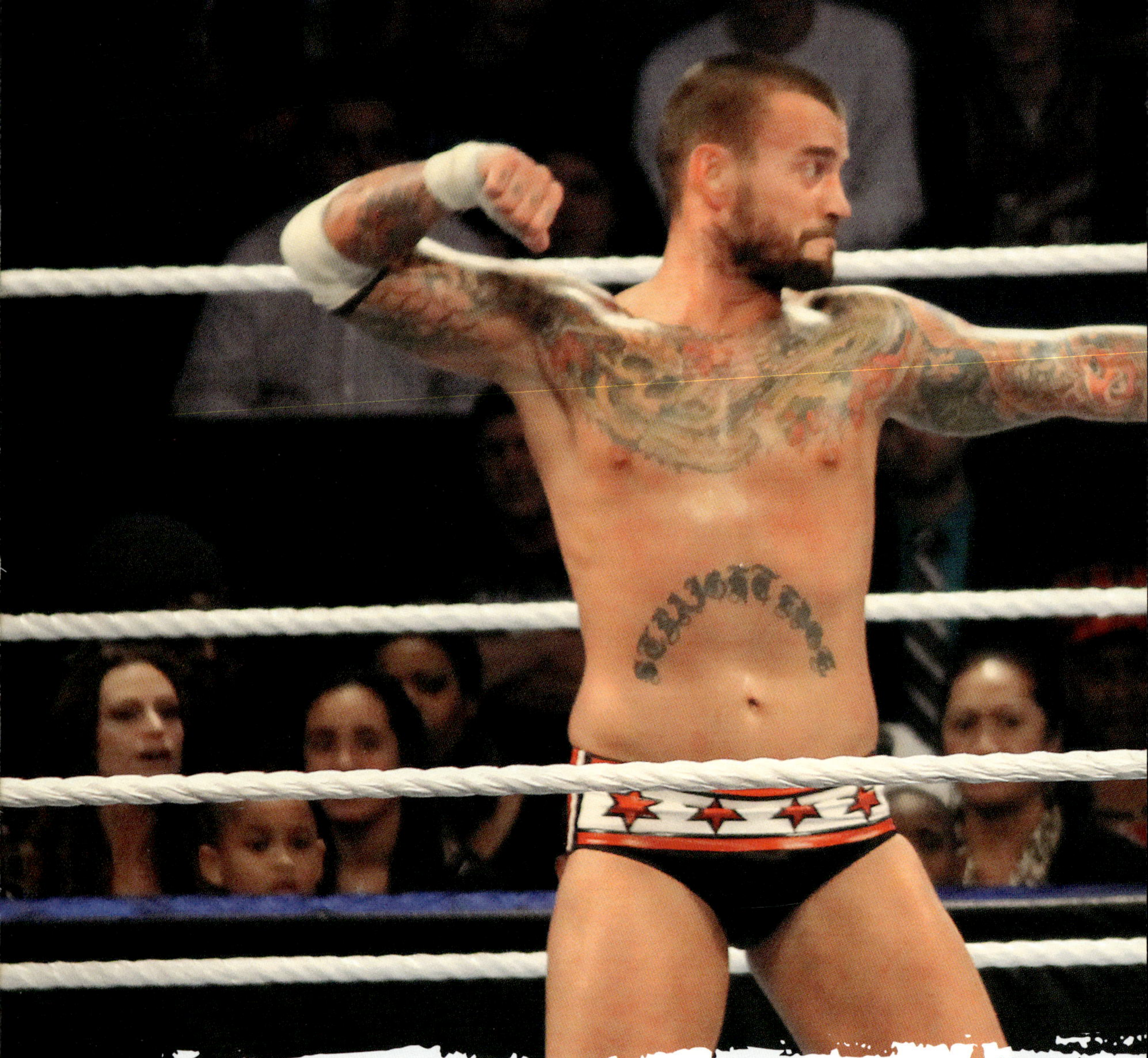

As a teenager, Dwayne tried to be good, but he often got into trouble. By the time he was 17, he had been arrested many times for fighting and stealing. When Dwayne attended high school in Pennsylvania, he met Jody Cwik,

When the Rock fought CM Punk (*left*) in 2013, he almost lost. But in the end he defeated his rival.

the school's football coach. Cwik took a chance on Dwayne and persuaded him to play football. Through football, Dwayne learned the importance of hard work, **discipline**, and **perseverance**.

In 2007, Johnson and his first wife, Dany Johnson, gave a gift of $1 million to the University of Miami to help fix its football facilities.

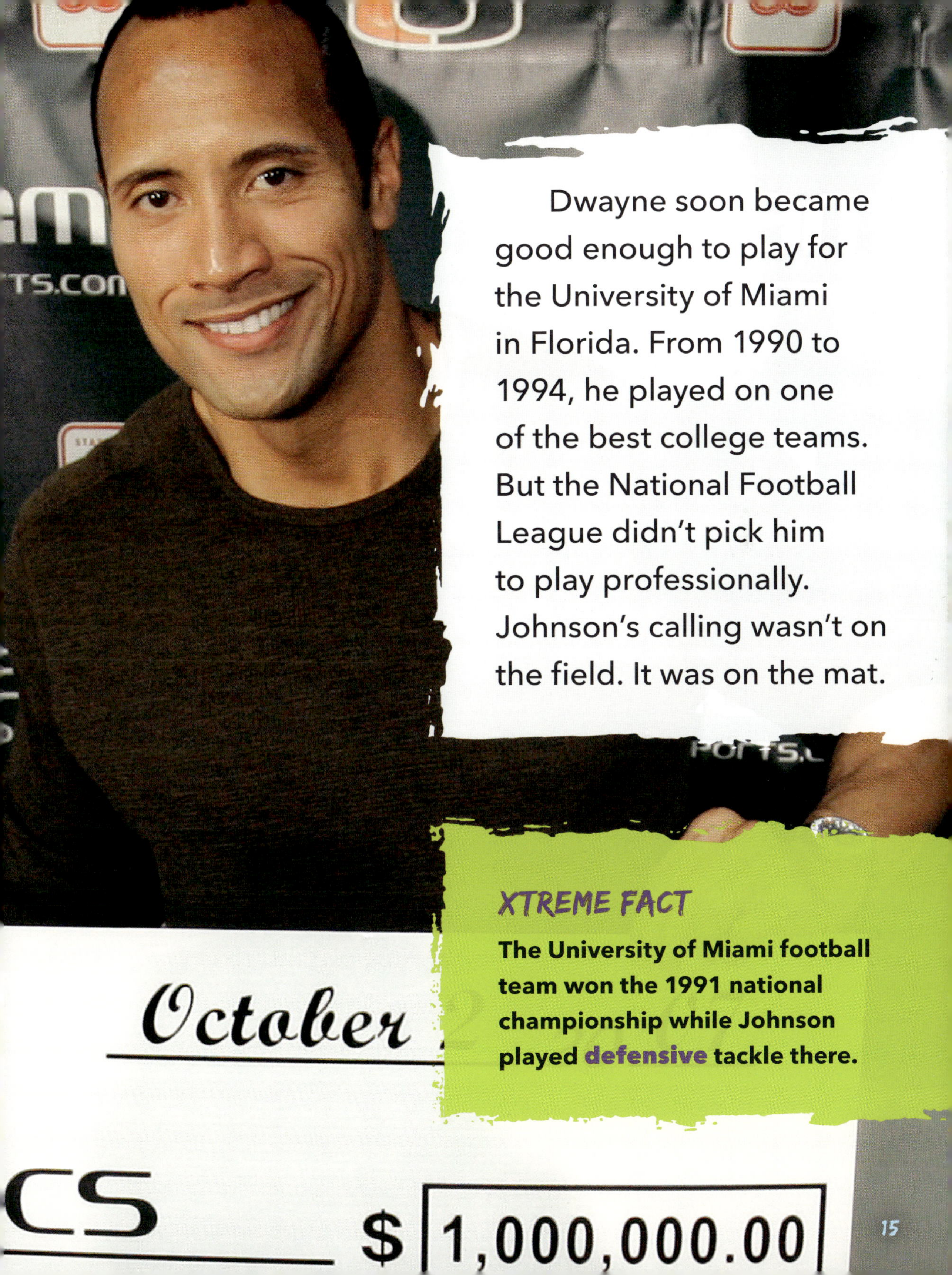

Dwayne soon became good enough to play for the University of Miami in Florida. From 1990 to 1994, he played on one of the best college teams. But the National Football League didn't pick him to play professionally. Johnson's calling wasn't on the field. It was on the mat.

XTREME FACT

The University of Miami football team won the 1991 national championship while Johnson played defensive tackle there.

CHAPTER 4

FAMILY FOOTSTEPS

After leaving football, Johnson started training with his father. Johnson was wrestling at flea markets for $40 a show by 1996. Later that year, the WWF offered Johnson a contract.

XTREME FACT

The WWF became the WWE in 2002. It is a professional wrestling organization that features characters who perform in staged matches.

Johnson defeated opponent Erick Rowan (*center*) in six seconds during WrestleMania XXXII in 2016. It was a record for the fastest win in WrestleMania history.

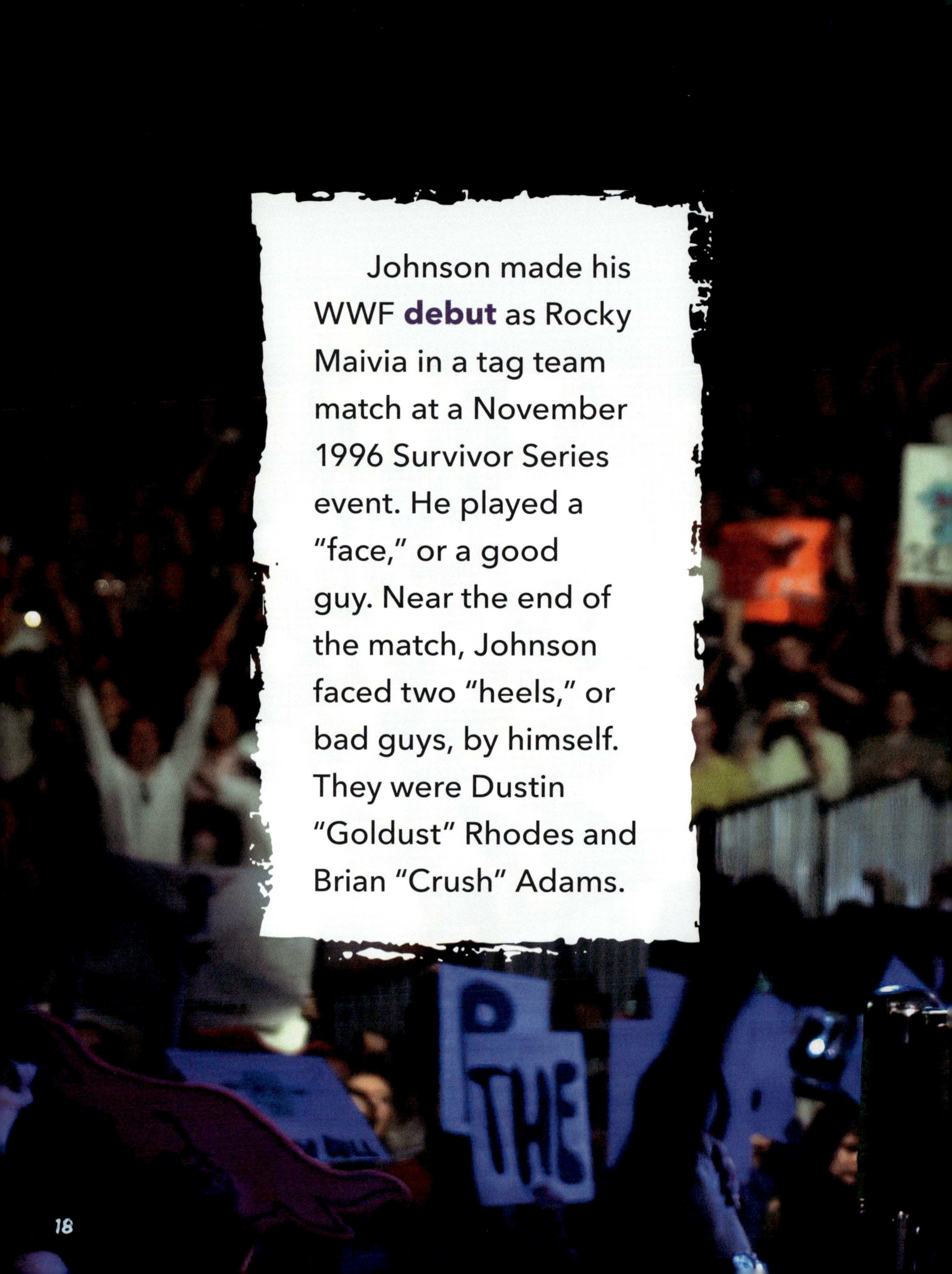

Johnson made his WWF **debut** as Rocky Maivia in a tag team match at a November 1996 Survivor Series event. He played a "face," or a good guy. Near the end of the match, Johnson faced two "heels," or bad guys, by himself. They were Dustin "Goldust" Rhodes and Brian "Crush" Adams.

Johnson's nickname Rocky Maivia was a mix of his father's and grandfather's names.

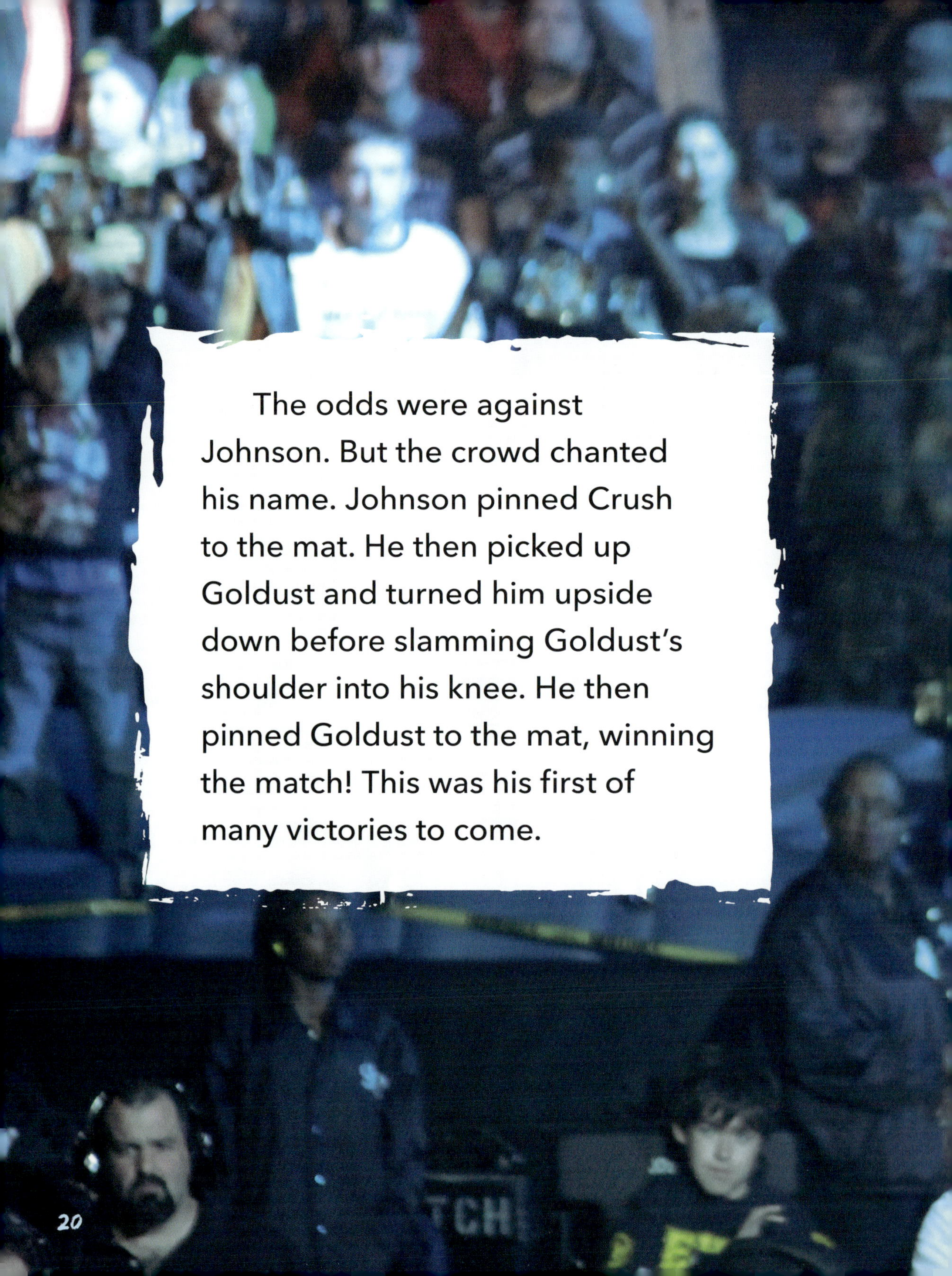

The odds were against Johnson. But the crowd chanted his name. Johnson pinned Crush to the mat. He then picked up Goldust and turned him upside down before slamming Goldust's shoulder into his knee. He then pinned Goldust to the mat, winning the match! This was his first of many victories to come.

Johnson has a signature pose that he uses before his wrestling matches and after the matches when he wins.

XTREME FACT

Johnson's daughter Simone Johnson is also going into wrestling. In 2022, she announced she would wrestle as Ava Raine.

CHAPTER 5

DISHING UP ATTITUDE

In February 1997, Johnson won the WWF Intercontinental Championship. But his popularity soon fell because he acted too nice. The WWF was entering the **Attitude** Era, a period of time where the WWF featured more adult-themed content. Even the WWF's good guys used foul language and ignored the rules. Many fans loved this content, and the WWF became more popular than ever.

Johnson won the Intercontinental Championship from Hunter Hearst Helmsley at Monday Night Raw.

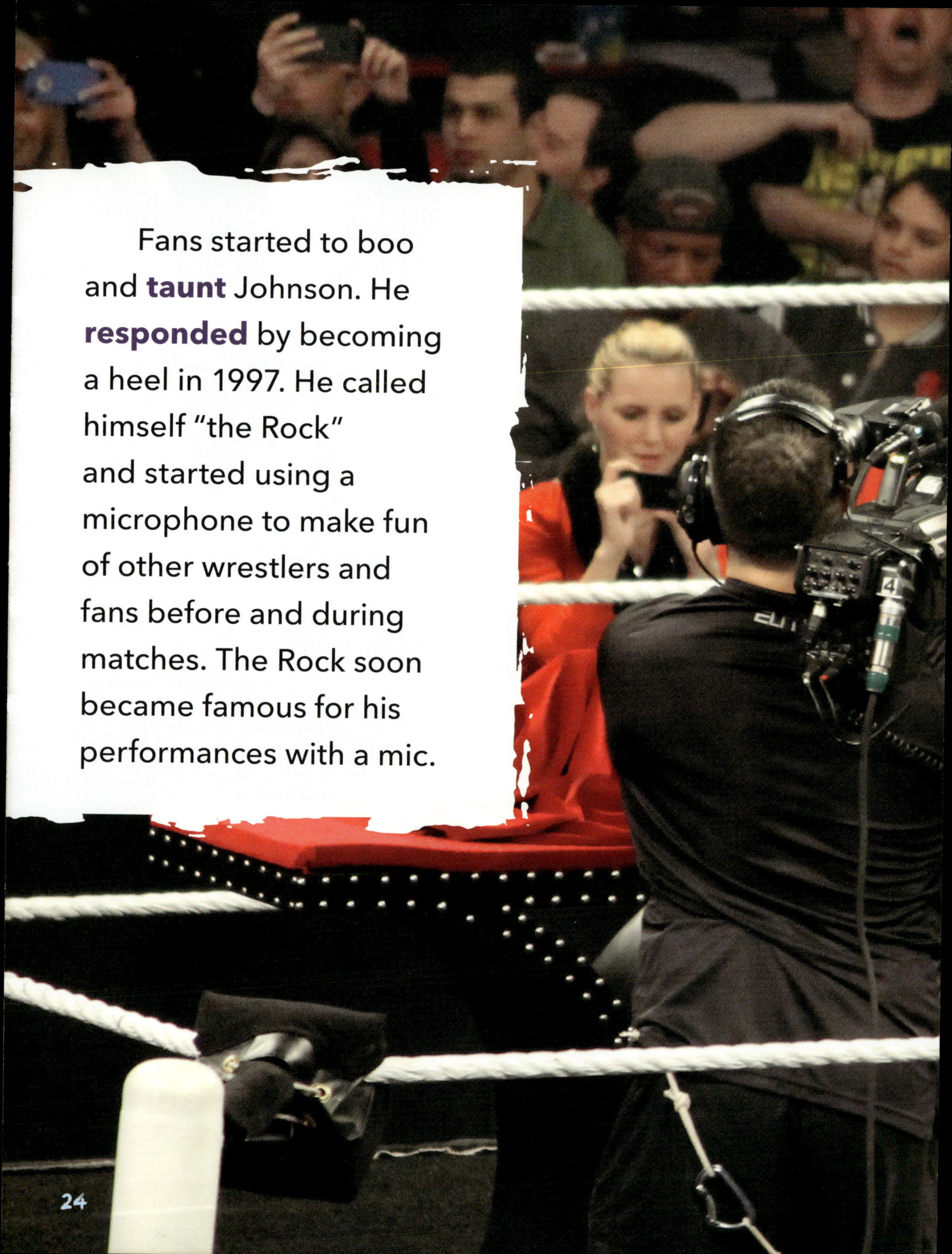

Fans started to boo and **taunt** Johnson. He **responded** by becoming a heel in 1997. He called himself "the Rock" and started using a microphone to make fun of other wrestlers and fans before and during matches. The Rock soon became famous for his performances with a mic.

The Rock loved entertaining WWF fans with "Rock Concerts." He would mock WWF performers and fans in his songs.

The Rock uses the People's Eyebrow move while at the Teen Choice Awards in California in 2001.

The Rock's WWF **personality** continued to grow. He invented the People's Eyebrow. He would lift one eyebrow and lower the other while staring at his opponents. He also began saying "Do ya smell what the Rock is cookin'?" This **catchphrase** became known around the world.

XTREME FACT

The Rock also called himself "the People's Champion" in honor of Muhammad Ali, who used the same nickname. Ali was a famous boxer and is one of the biggest sports superstars ever.

The WWF named Johnson "the Most Electrifying Man in Sports Entertainment." Johnson proved this by setting fire to a "Rock" sign during WrestleMania XXXII.

CHAPTER 6

FINDING FAME

The Rock (*center*) used his move, the People's Elbow, on Erick Rowan (*bottom*) during WrestleMania XXXII.

WrestleMania XXXII

The Rock had an entertaining **personality**, but he also had some famous wrestling moves. One was the People's Elbow. The Rock threw his elbow pad into the crowd before **bouncing** off the ropes to deliver an elbow drop onto his opponent. Another fan favorite was the Rock Bottom Chokeslam. The Rock would lift his opponent and throw him onto the mat.

The Rock gained more rivals as his popularity increased. He became a face again as he **feuded** with heel Paul "Triple H" Levesque. "Stone Cold" Steve Austin beat the Rock in several fights for

the World Heavyweight Championship during their rivalry. And the Rock's 1998 Survivor Series victory started a feud with Mankind that lasted until 1999.

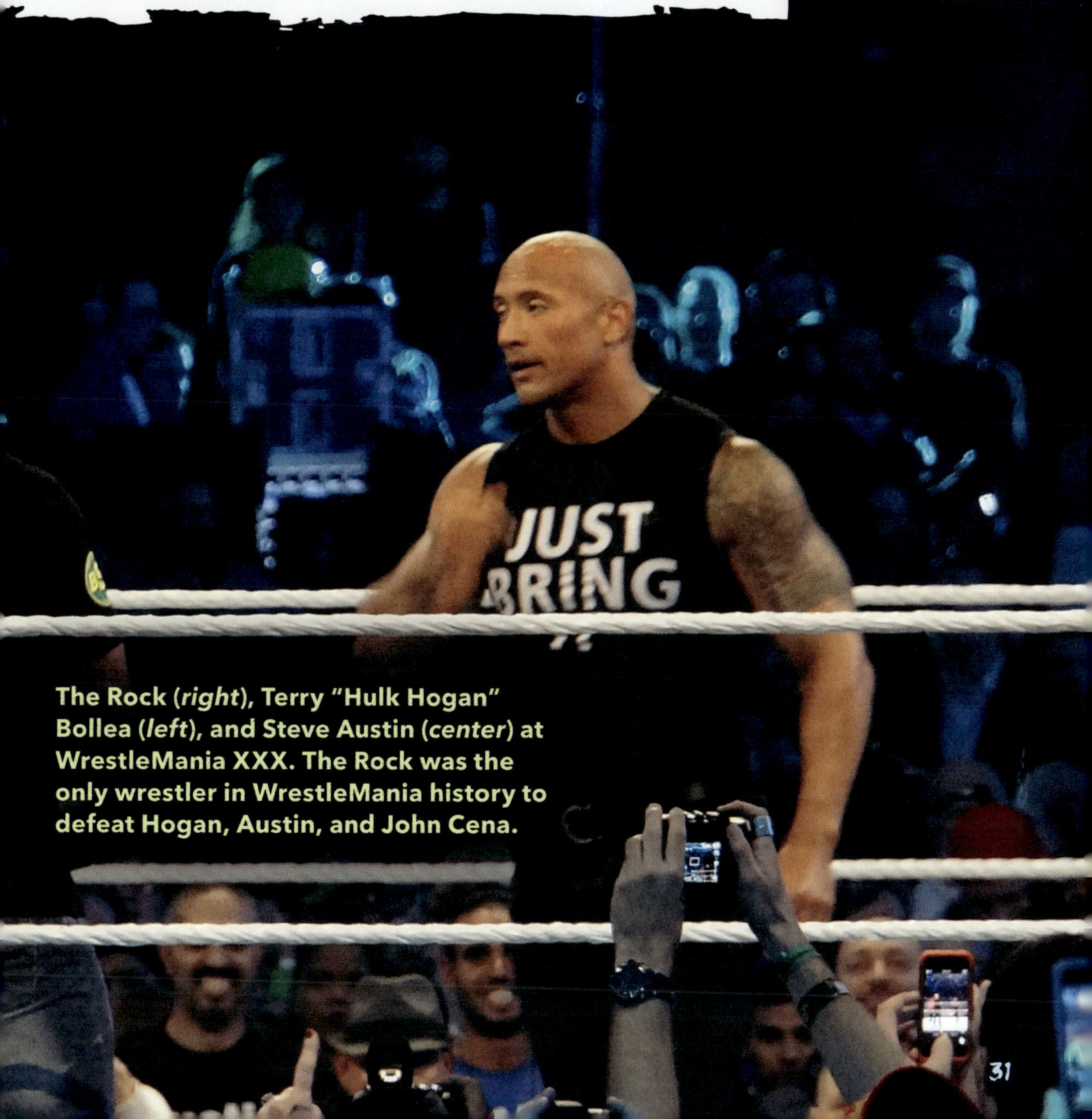

The Rock (*right*), Terry "Hulk Hogan" Bollea (*left*), and Steve Austin (*center*) at WrestleMania XXX. The Rock was the only wrestler in WrestleMania history to defeat Hogan, Austin, and John Cena.

JUST
BRING
IT

After his **feud** with Mankind, the Rock became a heel again, joined a wrestling team called the Corporation, and was named the Corporate Champion. But he was so entertaining, fans still loved him.

XTREME FACT

The Rock won his first WWF Championship at the 1998 Survivor Series event. He was 26 and a half years old, making him the second youngest champion in the WWF at the time.

The Rock stands over Phillip "CM Punk" Brooks in victory during WWE Raw.

CHAPTER 7

CAN'T KEEP A CHAMPION DOWN

The Rock didn't stay with the Corporation for long. In 1999, he partnered with Mankind. They won three WWF Tag Team Championships as the Rock 'n' Sock Connection. But the Rock also wrestled on his own. Between 1998 and 2002, the Rock won the WWF Championship seven times.

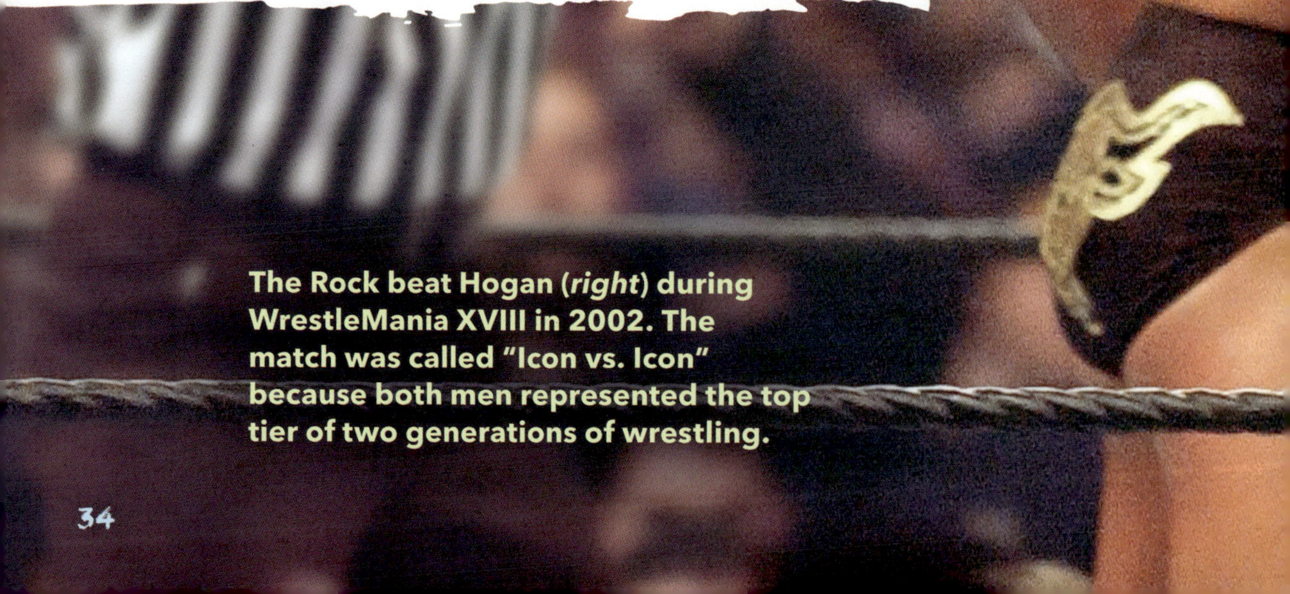

The Rock beat Hogan (*right*) during WrestleMania XVIII in 2002. The match was called "Icon vs. Icon" because both men represented the top tier of two generations of wrestling.

In 2004, the Rock retired from WWE to be an actor. But he missed wrestling. So he returned to WWE in 2011 and started a **feud** with superstar John Cena. In 2012, they fought at WrestleMania XXVIII. WrestleMania is one of WWE's most important and popular annual events. The Rock hit Cena with two Rock Bottom Chokeslam moves, winning the match.

When the Rock defeated Cena during WrestleMania XXVIII, it was the Rock's first WrestleMania Main Event win.

In 2013, the Rock won the WWE Championship for the eighth time. Cena defeated the Rock at WrestleMania XXIX in April, winning the championship. After that, the Rock retired from wrestling again.

The Rock's WrestleMania XXVIII match against Cena (*bottom*) was his most famous match in nine years. At the time, the event was also the highest grossing in WWE history.

CHAPTER 8

BIG-SCREEN SUPERSTAR

The Rock gives a speech as he receives a star on the Hollywood Walk of Fame.

In 2017, the Hollywood Chamber of Commerce honored the Rock with a star on the Hollywood Walk of Fame.

The Rock is wrestling royalty. But he's also a huge movie star. He has appeared in action, comedy, drama, and superhero films. His movies have earned billions of dollars in ticket sales around the world.

The Rock and his second wife, Lauren Hashian, at a *Moana* screening.

XTREME FACT

The Rock also produced a comedy show based on his childhood called *Young Rock*. The show first aired in February 2021.

In 1999, the Rock made his first TV guest appearance. His first lead **role** was the Scorpion King in the 2001 film *The Mummy Returns*. He's since played an explorer, a CIA agent, and an **antihero**. He also voiced the character Maui in the 2016 movie *Moana*.

The role of Maui in *Moana* gave the Rock a chance to share his Polynesian culture with the world. The character was also partially inspired by his grandfather (*right*).

CHAPTER 9

AN UNFORGETTABLE ICON

After 2013, the Rock appeared at a few different WWE events before retiring again in 2019. He is a wrestling **legend** to many fans. The Rock's performances on the microphone took his career to new heights. And he continues to entertain fans around the world.

XTREME CHALLENGE

TAKE THE QUIZ BELOW AND PUT WHAT YOU'VE LEARNED TO THE TEST!

1) Who was the Rock's tag team partner in the Rock 'n' Sock Connection?

2) What do you think are the benefits of playing sports in school?

3) Do you like to cheer for wrestlers who are heels or faces?

4) What was the Rock's first wrestling name in the WWF?

5) What was the Rock's famous catchphrase?

GLOSSARY

antihero–a central character in a story, movie, or drama who does not have heroic qualities.

attitude–the way someone thinks or feels about something.

bounce–to spring up or back after hitting something.

catchphrase–a well-known sentence or phrase.

debut–a first appearance.

defensive–related to keeping the other team from scoring in a game.

determination–firm or fixed intention.

discipline–training that molds, corrects, or perfects something.

feud–a long-lasting fight or disagreement.

induct–to admit as a member.

legend–a famous or important person, place, or thing that is known for doing something very well.

perseverance—the quality that allows a person to keep trying to do something even though it is difficult.

personality—the special characteristics of a person.

respond—to react to something.

role—a part played by an actor.

stunt—an unusual or daring action used to gain attention.

taunt—to provoke or challenge with insulting remarks.

ONLINE RESOURCES

Booklinks
NONFICTION NETWORK
FREE! ONLINE NONFICTION RESOURCES

To learn more about Dwayne "the Rock" Johnson, please visit **abdobooklinks.com** or scan this QR code. These links are routinely monitored and updated to provide the most current information available.

INDEX